Learn About the TOWN

Coloring Book

Written by Kaori Crutcher
Illustrated by C.A. Nobens

FS144010 Learn About the Town

23740 Hawthorne Blvd., Torrance, CA 90505

Name ____

A Busy Town

There are lots of people and places to see around a town.

Name ____

A Neighborhood

Your neighborhood is the place you call home.

Name ____

Main Street

Many towns have a central street called Main Street.

Name ________________________________

Police Station

The police station is the headquarters of the police force.

Name ____

Police Officers

Police officers work to keep our cities and towns safe.

Name ______________________________

Fire Station

The fire station is the building where firefighters work.

Name ______________________________

Firefighters

Firefighters rush to fires and put them out.

Name ______________________________

Store

Salespeople sell merchandise in a store.

Name ___________________________________

Restaurant

You can order your favorite meal in a restaurant.

Name ________________________________

Chefs

Chefs prepare food in the kitchen of a restaurant.

Name ____________________

Bank

A bank is a place that receives and lends money.

Name ______________________________

Grocery Store

Grocery stores have many different foods to buy.

Name ____________________

Library

A library is a place where you can go to borrow books.

Name ______________________________

Librarians

Librarians read stories and help people find books.

Name ____

School

A school is a place where people go to learn.

Name ____________________

Teachers

Teachers help people learn.

Name ______________________________

Airport

An airport is a place where airplanes take off and land.

Name ____

Bakery

Many towns have a bakery where baked goods are sold.

Name ______________________________

Parades

Towns often have parades on holidays.

Name ____

Post Office

A post office is a place where mail is processed.

Name ____________________

Mail Carriers

Mail carriers deliver mail to homes and businesses.

Name ____

A hospital is a place where sick people are treated.

Name ______________________________

Doctors and Nurses

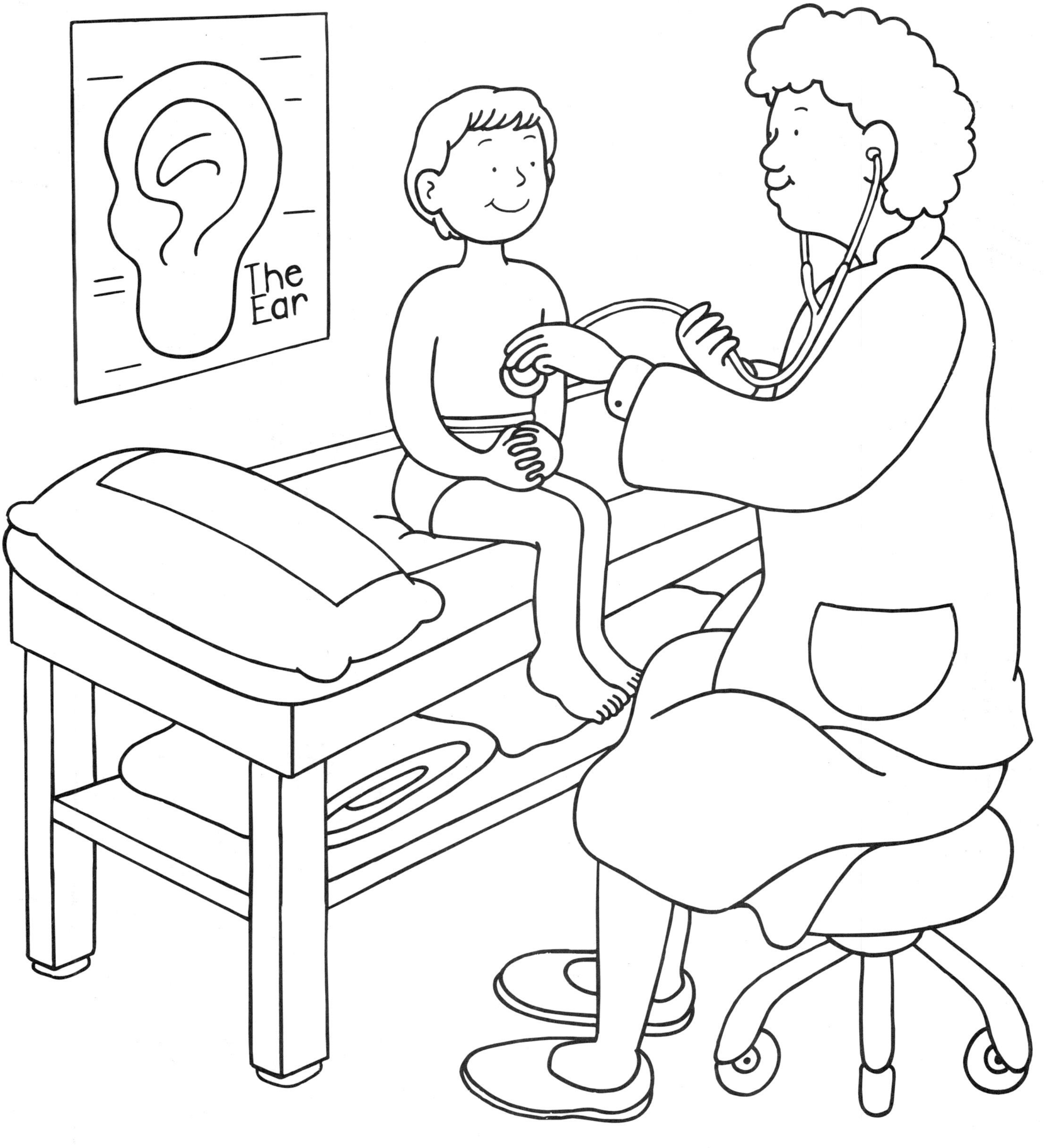

Doctors and nurses help to heal people who are sick.

Name ____________________

Dentists

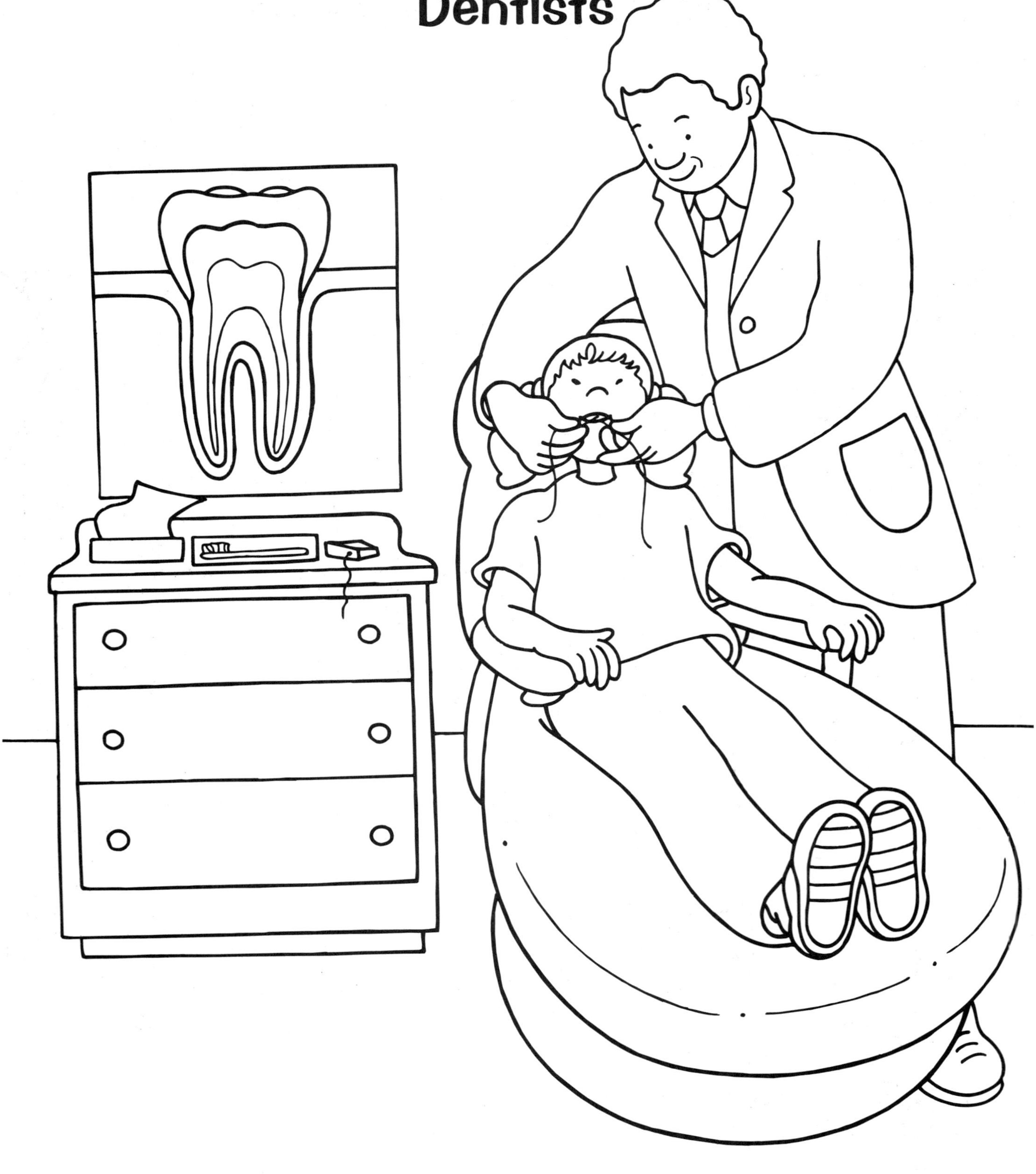

Dentists are doctors who care for our teeth.

Name ___________________________________

Construction Workers

Construction workers build houses and buildings in a town.

Name ____

Taxi Drivers

Taxi drivers charge a fare to drive people around.

Name ____

Sanitation Workers

Sanitation workers take away garbage from neighborhoods.

Name ______________________________

Gardeners

Gardeners take care of yards to make them look nice.

Name ____________________

Hairdressers

Hairdressers cut and take care of people's hair.

Name ____

Town Park

Many towns have a park where people can enjoy nature.